Marketing Fear for Fun and Profit

They'll Buy or They'll Die!

The Condensed Version

By Steve Germain

ISBN-13: 9781499629873

People fear what they don't understand. So, it's on you to make them understand what to fear.

First, create and plant the most frightening, "this is the worst thing that can ever, ever happen to me" scenario in the consumer's mind.

Next, deliver the perfect solution or at least the perfect *perceived* solution (for a nominal fee).

You have now achieved instant hero status (meaning sales, cash, unconditional love, sex, drugs and/or R & R).

Make Fear-Based Marketing Work for You

Create their worst fear, dread and panic in pictures, words, scenarios and soundtrack.

Then sell them happy calm and perceived personal security through your instant solutions.

Only thing to do next is decide where to roll that

wheelbarrow of cash. Pretty simple if you think about it. Let's talk about some current fear ad concepts that are currently floating around like logs in the toilet:

- I can't get an erection to screw my wife/girlfriend/boyfriend/pet burro but you say your product will make my dick hard and save my life and relationship. (But not for more than four consecutive hours or I may pop like an overstuffed burrito?) Swell, sign me up!

- You can stop my suicide-enducing, menstruation crotch leakage while I do flips off the diving board? Super duper!

- I can spray paint the hole in my boat with automobile undercoating and float my fat ass like a she cow over Niagara Falls while goat fairies strum their lutes in symphonic bliss and I won't get wet or sink? You sir are my savior!

Okay. Fine. Great. That's swell. We've all seen this shit but why is it that we recall these pitches long afterward? Because they address a fear and get people to buy. Marketing fear works.

But let's get down to brass tacks.

To quote: "Re Ipsa Loquitur."

"The Thing Speaks for Itself."

Positive ad campaigns do have their place and that

place is firmly entrenched in the sappy bleeding hearts and mashed potato minds of not only the backboneless business executive collective, but, especially and more specifically, Generic Consumer John/Jane Q. Public and his/her wallet.

That is... until the next ad, catch phrase, jingle, etc. that they'll see, hear, read or experience within the three seconds following your very expensive ad kicks your happy smiley, saccharine ad dollars to the curb where they die a slow, expensive yet so called "creative" death.

But this death is easily explainable by your current social media intern, experienced ad account manager, Creative Team Red or Creative Team Blue or Creative Team FU Leader, your pro-noid change agent yes-nodding bobbleheads or whomever it is spending your marketing dollars on doughy crap that they can be easily justified just by showing you your smiling face on a YouTube video.

I'm not angry. Not bitter. No Texas Clocktower or human skinlamps for me. I'm realistic. I'm the guy who can take a new business dreamer, a beaten-down middle product manager, or a completely inept and out-of-touch CEO and makes them appear smart, effective and a helper of all humanity.

After 30 years of magically congering words and phrases to elicit response – meaning writing marketing copy on a blank computer screen – I've learned what actually works in the real world and what a complete waste of money is. And by money I mean your freaking marketing budget that no one else in your company believes is a worthwhile expenditure except you.

What works, what really works, is a simple, exactingly exhaustive and explicit ploy you see everyday in the media:

Their worst fear is helplessness. Death lurks under their bed while they're unable to move. There really is a monster inside your child's closet or lunchbox or doll.

Through marketing fear the potential horrors we just made told you about become very, very real and ready and waiting to fuck your life to the core.

"But wait! We can solve all your problems…"

Chapter 1: Create the Fear

I absolutely love the mainstream media, marketing managers, advertising creatives, and everything sales related. I mean I absolutely love these rudderless fucks. They shill "perception is reality" at its best. I've used that mantra from the first job I had out of college and it continues to be instilled front and center in every piece I've ever written for any variety of client, client budget and client goal.

Almost all of the media relies on some level of fear to get eyes and pique interest. But does the panic/peril/ solution marketing concept resonate with that fat lump of humanity who has melted into the couch? The one that you're trying to motivate to act the way you want them to act?

You bet it does! Let me clarify. YOU BET YOUR FUCKING ASS IT DOES!

But, and listen to me now but hear me later, creating fear and panic takes a deft touch. The typical message is you know that certain death is imminent, here's exactly what to fear and now we'll sell you when, why or how to avoid it. Just call...

The Birth of Fear – Case Study I in Repose: Toilet Paper

Everyone craps. Does the Pope shit in the woods? Not sure, but I bet he only craps floaters shaped like crosses. Toilet issues are really not in the male domain because men crap on a schedule like a Swiss watch – the internal timer goes ding, sit, read, plop, wipe. But even men like a soft, familiar wipe.

But women fear the toilet, toilet paper and crap at random and often at very inopportune times such as exactly to the inch the mid-point between exits on the longest stretch of any highway on earth.

Crap in the woods? "Never."

Out-the-car-window-brown-flag-a-flying-at-speed? "Our relationship is over dear."

Crap at the immigrant Bodega? "Never."

Pinch a petite loaf in luxury at the recognizable fast food restaurant? "Maybe.

"But wait!?! What of the toilet paper!? It must be of the exact brand I use at home or I'll hold it until I swell up with a poop-baby belly and you will bear the full fury of my misery!"

No single ply creation on earth evokes as much heartfelt love, admiration, dread, fear and panic as much as toilet paper. But the key is to make your uber emotional pitch – good is good but fear/panic/solution drives real sales – work for you in the most effective, spring fresh and butt-Klingon-free way.

By marketing to fear and peril you paint the picture of how your target market's life will be worse, embarrassing, do-do stained and smelly if they don't get the product in you're pitching.

And not just any product – your specific brand of product. Anything else could blowtorch you and/or your butt, end your relationship, ensure that your kids appear in a "Gone Wild" video, blot out your future and eliminate your current status in Heaven or Hell depending.

Ahh the toilet paper. No cute, animated baby bear crapping in the woods will make you want to wipe you ass with that product. The right tact is panic marketing at it's best. Use our paper or your ass will make you pay a heavy, heavy price.

Case Study Dos: Kill my Dog, Please!

"Oh crap, little yippy Spot got off the leash, tried to hump a porcupine and shisk-ka-bobbed himself to death."

Like this, the death-marketing message for your product must play into existing fears to be effective just like this little gem.

Maybe you can create a new uncertainty that consumers may never have considered to be a threat in their sedate, ant-farm lives.

Maybe you can take a serene Norman Rockwell event and show that the worst can happen during happy happy times.

The end result of any fear marketing message is that the derived perception/reality of your product or service is an abject necessity to keep John Doe or, even better because she controls the purse strings, Mrs. Doe, and her family safe, make their lives better and/or mitigate the very situation that creates the maximum dread in their hearts and minds.

That maximum dread is, of course, the one you just planted in their minds.

I've Fallen and... I Can't Believe You Aren't

Helping Me You Fucking Rotten Kid! (*and Grandma then died*)

I saw this enduring and endearing TV ad a few minutes ago and it actually motivated me to write this book.

What are the primary messages of this ad campaign and what fear/solution messages does it leave in your mind?

It paints a direct, graphic picture of what your, your mother's, and/or your grandmother's life might be like if you don't buy the product and right now.

It creates the perception that this product is an absolute necessity to keep your family safe, avoid a situation that's universally dreaded and ultimately make everyone's life better and happier.

It crosses the line on a morally questionable strategy (grandma is fish flopping on the floor without help and you're to blame you rotten child!), but when it ends with a positive solution, all is forgiven.

But doesn't fear marketing weaken society as a whole by creating false insecurities and sending massively negative messages to the world? Yes, probably. But who the fuck are you, Gandhi? You aren't here to save the world you're in business to move product. But the fact remains that however reprehensible marketing fear works which is why it's so prevalent.

The Slippery Slope of Marketing Fear for Profit Messaging

Because fear marketing can go horribly wrong when it is not carried out in the most precisely professionally planned way, suggestions on how to make any death/fear/panic-based marketing campaign more effective follow:

1. Always, always offer a specific solution that your target market can easily understand and that will prevent the horrible thing that is about to happen. If your fear-based marketing presents a clear and present danger without giving the audience a way to make everything better, you've created helplessness and negativity. But, by providing a clear course of remedy (meaning your product or service) that the person can buy and use, you're now the hero making their lives better.

2. Be sure that the portrayed peril is a believable and understandable event that could easily happen in everyday life. If the peril is too exaggerated you will lose

credibility and not be taken seriously. A house roof leak, fixed with common car undercoating found at every auto parts store, will not also eliminate identify theft.

3. Ensure that the fear is real and relevant. The world can be a pretty bad place (film at 11!) and people are crushed by the scary images they see all day, every day. Show your audience that the peril you're trying to save them from can and does happen to people just like them. They will be much more likely to pay attention because you've told them why they should care, how the issue relates to their lives and what your solution is.

The more effectively you can relate personally relevant information to your audience the more likely they are to buy your product or service. But enter death-based marketing campaigns at your own risk!

Chapter 2: Sunshine Wafts From My Butt

You and you alone can solve the problem that you've are creating in the minds of your soon-to-be customers. You are the problem solver. You make life better. You are on their side. You are only here to help them (at $19.99 per unit, but wait...).

Step 1: Tell Them They Have a Problem

Ultimately your message must persuade the user to take specific action and you can only accomplish this by making sure they know they have a problem.

To motivate anyone to do anything you have to convince them that what they need is missing and that you can provide it (or your money back – *not really*).

15

You are in the problem-solving business and you have to convince the populace to say, "I've got to get me some of that."

Tell Them What to Think

- Convince people that the problem you solve is the worst horror on earth.
- Convince buyers that this problem will affect them personally and not just their neighbors. "Not my problem" or "Not me" are arguments you have to hurdle.
- Convince people that the doom is imminent.
- Convince people that the steps you suggest will save them.
- Convince them with an immediate closing statement such as "call now."
- Convince people that you can help them live a better life, be more popular, be richer, bigger tits, bigger dick, live longer, look better, or any other vanity or fear they have.

Counter Their Arguments Upfront

Everyone is a skeptic so nip that shit in the bud before they can every get their concerns percolating.

The arguments to overcome:

- It's too expensive.
- Tried that before – didn't work

- Doesn't apply to me.
- Don't need it.

Your Answers:

- Our product is more effective previous, similar products and here's how.
- Our solution is easier to use.
- You owe it to yourself to try our improved version.
- The price is nothing compared to how much better your life will be.
- You are directly affected in these ways.
- You will fucking die if you don't buy!

Very Successful Fear-Based Campaigns
Subaru: "They Lived"

Subaru has a history of great safety ratings dating back many years but no one really cared unless you lived in Colorado and celebrated April 20 like a national holiday.

Listing their safety features, ratings and history in a brochure wasn't going to do anything – you had to see, feel and want the safety they were offering.

So they created a fear-based ad campaign that showed that, if you didn't drive their car your entire family will be killed in a car accident. This is what their cars were all about and if you don't drive one you're dead and your family is dead.

Pretty clear message wouldn't you say?

Their marketing images and messaging are real, gripping and hit home with anyone who has ever been part of a family and leaves viewers with an etched image of Subaru safety in their mind.

What makes this campaign great is the fact that it reveals your true fears about car wrecks. Accidents can kill you and your family. Want to live? Drive a fucking Subaru. I'm sold.

Listerine: "What You Don't Know Can Kill You"

"What the hell is halitosis and how is it ruining my life? Ahhhhhh!"

Well, Listerine told you. They became successful by scaring people to death with the term chronic halitosis. You know what halitosis is? Bad breath.

Beginning in the early 1900's and continuing in campaigns today Listerine advertised bad breath as a deal breaker when trying to find love and also a potential health hazard.

Bad breath? Better click YouPorn cuz you ain't getting any.

They said that everyone with bad breath wasn't going to find love in their life and that fear was enough to establish Listerine as the source for this fresh breath and not loneliness, blue balls or old maids by halitosis.

Smoke up Johnny! Feeding the Addiction.

No one really wants to face the whole truth. Here's fear marketing that tackled a tough market – addicted assholes. "I smoked and now I talk out of a fucking tube in my throat. Check out my amputated leg. Pretty cool, huh? Be like me..."

The truth is that people are idiots and also that people are addicted to a variety of things.

After years of telling, and showing, the American people how they are uncool and weak unless they smoke cigarettes the manufacturers were forced through litigation to fund anti-smoking campaigns and associated PSAs.

Truth.com knew that it couldn't give the same tired "Just say no" bullshit. To get people to stop smoking Truth made ads that showed the harsh reality that no rebellious teenager would think was cool.

Most teens may not understand nor care if they get cancer from smoking but most of them sure don't want to be thinking about having half a leg when they light up that square.

This specific fear-based marketing campaign shows that they understood their target market and took a dramatically different and specific angle to get the message to hit home.

Can you also take such a dramatic approach to sway hearts and minds to your product? Absolutely!

Chapter 3: We Can Make You Live Forever. Ring/Ring... Hello, FTC!

When in Doubt, Be Vague

Your message is your product, your business, your Mojo, your big swinging dick (really a rolled up tube sock), your hypnotizing illusion of push-up cleavage, and ultimately the difference between making money and just being another fear-mongering asshole being fined for false advertising.

Further, how you craft your message will be the difference between becoming a perceived savior with your customers and getting a summons from the Man.

Here are some tips on how to properly phrase your message without attracting unwanted attention. NOTE:

These tips are simply ideas to consider.

How you create your business's message is your decision and we do encourage you to follow common sense.

Enjoy.

Truth in Advertising: Big Brother's a Knockin'

The ultimate heavyweight in the ring of false advertising regulation is the Federal Trade Commission (FTC). Beyond the Better Business Bureau, Angie's List, Google Rankings, and all the other business gossip and so-called oversight entities, really, only the FTC and the court system can hit you in the cajones if you cross the product promise line.

Here is what the Federal Trade Commission has to say on its website about false advertising messages:

Advertising FAQ's: A Guide for Small Business

What truth-in-advertising rules apply to advertisers? Under the Federal Trade Commission Act:

- Advertising must be truthful and non-deceptive;
- Advertisers must have evidence to back up their claims; and Advertisements cannot be unfair.

Additional laws apply to ads for specialized products like consumer leases, credit, 900 telephone numbers, and products sold through mail order or telephone sales. And every state has consumer protection laws that govern ads running in that state.

What makes an advertisement deceptive?

According to the FTC's Deception Policy Statement, an ad is deceptive if it contains a statement – or omits information – that:

- Is likely to mislead consumers acting reasonably under the circumstances; and
- Is "material" - that is, important to a consumer's decision to buy or use the product?

What makes an advertisement unfair?

According to the Federal Trade Commission Act and the FTC's Unfairness Policy Statement, an ad or business practice is unfair if:

- It causes or is likely to cause substantial consumer injury which a consumer could not reasonably avoid; and,
- It is not outweighed by the benefit to consumers.

How does the FTC determine if an ad is deceptive?

A typical inquiry follows these steps:

The FTC looks at the ad from the point of view of the "reasonable consumer" – the typical person looking at the ad. Rather than focusing on certain words, the FTC looks at the ad in context – words, phrases, and pictures – to determine what it conveys to consumers.

The FTC looks at both "express" and "implied" claims. An express claim is literally made in the ad. For example, "ABC Mouthwash prevents colds" is an express claim that the product will prevent colds.

An implied claim is one made indirectly or by

inference. "ABC Mouthwash kills the germs that cause colds" contains an implied claim that the product will prevent colds.

Although the ad doesn't literally say that the product prevents colds, it would be reasonable for a consumer to conclude from the statement "kills the germs that cause colds" that the product will prevent colds. Under the law, advertisers must have proof to back up express and implied claims that consumers take from an ad.

The FTC looks at what the ad does not say – that is, if the failure to include information leaves consumers with a misimpression about the product. For example, if a company advertised a collection of books, the ad would be deceptive if it did not disclose that consumers actually would receive abridged versions of the books.

The FTC looks at whether the claim would be "material" – that is, important to a consumer's decision to buy or use the product. Examples of material claims are representations about a product's performance, features, safety, price, or effectiveness.

The FTC looks at whether the advertiser has sufficient evidence to support the claims in the ad. The law requires that advertisers have proof before the ad runs.

What kind of evidence must a company have to support the claims in its ads?

Before a company runs an ad, it has to have a "reasonable basis" for the claims. A "reasonable basis" means objective evidence that supports the claim. The kind of evidence depends on the claim. At a minimum, an advertiser must have the level of evidence that it says it has. For example, the statement "Two out of three doctors recommend ABC Pain Reliever" must be supported by a reliable survey to that effect. If the ad isn't specific, the FTC looks at several factors to determine what level of proof is necessary, including what experts in the field think is needed to support the claim. In most cases, ads that make health or safety claims must be supported by "competent and reliable scientific evidence" – tests, studies, or other scientific evidence that has been evaluated by people qualified to review it. In addition, any tests or studies must be conducted using methods that experts in the field accept as accurate.

Are letters from satisfied customers sufficient to substantiate a claim?

No. Statements from satisfied customers usually are not sufficient to support a health or safety claim or any other claim that requires objective evaluation.

My company offers a money-back guarantee. Very few people have ever asked for their money back. Must we still have proof to support our advertising claims? Yes. Offering a money-back guarantee is not a substitute for substantiation. Advertisers still must have proof to support their claims.

What kind of advertising claims does the FTC focus on?

The FTC pays closest attention to:

Ads that make claims about health or safety, such as:

- ABC Sunscreen will reduce the risk of skin cancer.
- ABC Water Filters remove harmful chemicals from tap water.
- ABC Chainsaw's safety latch reduces the risk of injury.
- Ads that make claims that consumers would have trouble evaluating for themselves, such as:
- ABC Refrigerators will reduce your energy costs by 25%.
- ABC Gasoline decreases engine wear.
- ABC Hairspray is safe for the ozone.

Ads that make subjective claims or claims that consumers can judge for themselves (for example, "ABC Cola tastes great") receive less attention from the FTC.

How does the FTC decide what cases to bring?

The FTC weighs several factors, including:

FTC jurisdiction. Although the FTC has jurisdiction over ads for most products and services, Congress has given other government agencies the authority to investigate advertising by airlines, banks, insurance companies, common carriers, and companies that sell securities and commodities.

The geographic scope of the advertising campaign. The FTC concentrates on national advertising and usually refers local matters to state, county, or city agencies. The extent to which an ad represents a pattern of deception, rather than an individual dispute between a consumer and a business or a dispute between two competitors.

State or local consumer protection agencies or private groups such as the Better Business Bureau (BBB) often are in a better position to resolve disputes involving local businesses or local advertising.

To get the address and phone number of your state Attorney General's office, your local consumer agency, or the nearest BBB, check your telephone directory.

The amount of injury – to consumers' health, safety, or wallets – that could result if consumers rely on the deceptive claim.

The FTC concentrates on cases that could affect consumers' health or safety (for example, deceptive health claims for foods or over-the-counter drugs) or cases that result in widespread economic injury.

What penalties can be imposed against a company that runs a false or deceptive ad?

The penalties depend on the nature of the violation. The remedies that the FTC or the courts have imposed include:

Cease and desist orders. These legally-binding orders require companies to stop running the deceptive ad or engaging in the deceptive practice, to have substantiation for claims in future ads, to report periodically to FTC staff about the substantiation they have for claims in new ads, and to pay a fine of $16,000 per day per ad if the company violates the law in the future.

Civil penalties, consumer redress and other monetary remedies. Civil penalties range from thousands of dollars to millions of dollars, depending on the nature of the violation. Sometimes advertisers have been ordered to give full or partial refunds to all consumers who bought the product.

Corrective advertising, disclosures and other informational remedies. Advertisers have been required to take out new ads to correct the misinformation conveyed in the original ad, notify purchasers about deceptive claims in ads, include specific disclosures in future ads, or provide other information to consumers.

Will the FTC review my company's ads before they run to make sure that we've complied with the law?

FTC staff cannot clear your ads in advance. However, there is guidance to help you comply with the law. Information about advertising particular kinds of products (for example, foods, dietary supplements, or "environmentally friendly" merchandise), advertising credit, and guidelines for advertising on the Internet is available at www.ftc.gov.

What All This Bullshit Means

What all this bullshit means to you is that you have to be careful and calculated in how you describe, present and market your best-product-ever to the public.

The last thing you want to do while you're selling the cure for all ills is to draw the attention of the truth police.

Take a cue from the financial services firms. They never make a concrete promise while simultaneously giving veiled promises and perceived guarantees to make your life better.

Words such as these in the following list are great to include because you're not actually claiming that your product does exactly what you are saying it does, but you still implanting those fantasies of a utopian life in the minds of the consumer:

- May
- Can
- For Me It
- Friends Say
- It Makes Sense That
- Who Wouldn't Want (*Benefit Here*)
- Past Results Don't Indicate Future Results

Common sense is the key and the thought police are watching.

When in doubt, be vague.

Learn it!

Love it!

Live it!

Chapter 4: Spreading the Panic: DIY Marketing

Okay, so you've created a product that, if the general population doesn't purchase it, they will face the worst personal and possible horrors both real and the ones you've instilled in them.

But if you're a DIY'er with a limited budget how do you get the word out to tell the world how you'll soon be saving their lives with just one small cup of Kool-Aid? Infomercials? Fuck no!

Exploit the Internet!

I've worked in ad agencies. I've owned an ad agency. I've worked in all levels of marketing departments from boiler rooms to the most respected *Fortune 500* companies. And what have I learned?

What I've learned is that with the level of proficiency of the average citizen, of even the most basic computer/Internet user, and the availability of free software (the legit shit, not the torrent programs that will steal your credit card numbers without you knowing it), enables the masses to market-it-themselves and makes online fear marketing easy and massively cost effective. When done the right way.

To create a website and personal blog you can get a free template from WordPress that allows you to drag and drop images and text wherever you want.

Get immediate attention by putting a picture front and center on your Homepage of an adorable baby crawling at speed toward a flight of stairs and certain peril! Then add a line about how your "Baby Life Saver 3000" product will prevent that tragedy and will also allay any other fears you may face as a parent.

So, you can get your website template for free for easy design. There are also hundreds of sites to get free images and artwork.

Remember that when writing copy for your site the goal is, well of course sales and riches, but first to generate Google website search rankings. Being listed on Page One is critical. How many times do you flip to the second search page when looking for something? If you're a typical net surfer you look at Page One and Page One only.

To help with website rankings just look at how keywords and keywords phrases are used in the sites that come up first during random searches of products similar to yours.

These are your Google fuck-buddy friends-with-privileges phrases that can get your site noticed and get frightened customers ordering your best-since-sliced-bread product.

When ready, visit a website hosting company such as HostGator that can walk you through how to upload your site to the web and also help you go live on the Internet for about $100 a year.

The Blog: Reinforce the Fear

Almost every free website template comes complete with Blog functionality. The Blog can become your best friend, or, your worst enemy.

The truth is that 99 percent of blogs are poorly written, they suck, they serve no real purpose other than everyone is delusional enough to think that others value their opinions, and that clients don't read them.

In a business tool such as online marketing where any and all information is cheap and immediate message blur is inevitable and very real.

There is simply no way anyone can digest every marketing message they are barraged with. This is why a purpose-driven, SEO-whored out blog can be the arrow in your quiver of marketing strategies that actually works and creates real results.

Blog Writing 101: What To Do/Not To Do

1. **Don't Only Talk About You**. No one except your mother (and honestly not even her) gives a shit what you had for lunch or wants another installment on your dog's ball-licking follies. Readers want "you've told me my problem, my biggest fear waiting around the corner, now tell me what's in it for me and how you will make my life better."

   By keeping it relevant and SEO driven you're learning how a blog can become the great marketing tool that can make you more money and get customers.

2. **Don't Publish Blog Updates daily.** Again, don't kid yourself that anyone really wants your information. Unless there's breaking news that affects all of your target market posting blog entries just once a week is enough to get your name and information to clients without becoming an overbearing dick.

If things do come up, however, that affect a specific demographic you're farming and your product is the golden remedy, then immediate and repetitive blog posts do serve a purpose.

3. **Don't Write Only for Keywords and Word Count**. Beyond unreadable and obnoxious, cramming millions of keywords, keyword phrases and unnecessary words to pad your blog posts will ensure that you die a quick death with both Google and clients.

4. **Do Throw the Thesaurus in the Trash.** Jargon, business-speak, hot air and six-syllable words will drive your readers away like I did to my college roommate after $1 taco night at Senor Poops-a-Lot.

   Write like you're talking about the worst that can happen to the reader and then write about how you can help. Simple, understandable messages written in plain, fear-driven English will keep interest which keeps readers reading which converts clicks into business.

5. **Do Know Thy Client – Know Their Fears.** Your business doesn't have to cure all ills on earth (just the worst one you're trying to make money off of) so don't write about everything on

earth. People go to your site because you offer something specific they need.

Deliver that something specific and get that cash flow.

The Truth About Blogs

- People don't give a fuck about you, only what you can do for them and do it now.
- People don't need another blog to read.
- A professional blog writer can make the difference between feast and famine.
- Everyone's time is precious, especially yours.

When it's Time to Call a Professional

If you do find yourself needing help writing your site/blog never, ever go to traditional advertising, marketing and public relations firms. Do an online search for a freelance copywriter who has proven success in writing direct response online copy plus SEO proficiency.

Why Use a Freelance Writer?

The basic truth is that if you need on-point, on-time and on-budget copywriting without the hot air, mystery billings and blown deadline excuses, a freelance writer is the only way to go. Here's why:

Agency Writer vs. Freelancer Writer

Ad Agency: Remember that an ad agency

copywriter is usually 5th in line to hear about and try to comprehend your true aim and goals. With an ad agency writer you first are paying for your ad rep's salary, paying for an art director's salary whether or not they are part of the process, paying for upper management's 401(k) and who knows what else is buried in your fee.

Freelance Copywriter: With a freelance copywriter you get dedication, personal service and someone who listens first and then acts. There are no layers between you and your freelance writer. Accountability is built in and undeniable because you are dealing directly with your writer and there are no smoke and mirrors. You pay for results only and results are what you want in the first place.

Agency Client Churn vs. Personal Service

Ad Agency: More clients mean more profit regardless of satisfaction or services provided so many account reps give a sales pitch telling you everything you want to hear.

This can lead to them claiming that their writers are experts in areas or industries where they have limited or no experience.

Further, if an ad agency is promising you an exact ROI or revenue stream that their copywriting will be generating they are simply lying to you.

Freelance Copywriter: Your freelance copywriter is the same person who picks up the phone when you call, the same person who works directly with you on changes to make your marketing as effective as possible, the same person you pay and the person who is accountable to you. Personal service.

Other DIY Tools: Use and Abuse the News Media!

The media includes newspapers, TV talking heads, local radio talk shows, print, online, on the air, live or tape delayed and every other prostitute supposedly giving you the real news. They are all fair game to help you get the word out about your potentially life-saving product and you can get them to talk about you for free if approached the right way. Who doesn't like free?

The media are basically blind sheep waiting for someone, anyone, to put a bucket of sensational slop in their trough so they have something to shit out and keep the fuzzy public's attention for a few seconds.

If they can pique the interest of the reader, viewer, online visitor or listener for four seconds or more then they become a trusted authority in hearts and minds of America which, in turn, translates into ratings which translates into what you and they are both in business for to begin with – profit.

But how do you get media exposure? A good start is a drool-inducing, frightening press release or local citizen testimonial story that they can exploit for ratings. Let's start with the press release.

The Press Release

One of the most cost effective, time efficient ways you can generate relevant, meaningful publicity (often good and/or bad publicity results in equal exposure) is the press release.

A press release, when written precisely and purpose-driven, can dictate what people will think, feel and say about your product through placement in the media with your message being front and center.

As stated with the marketing functions noted earlier, a professional freelance writer can put together PR pretty cheaply (again, fuck ad agency bullshit, hot air and layers of management), and shop it successfully to the media.

Want to try PR yourself? No worries. Go to any website of a company that either does what you do or simply is in the news all the time but this time search their "News" or "Investor Relations" tabs.

Here you can find templates to write your own PR from. Just copy the format with the contact info, text spacing and the "About Us" paragraph that ends 99 percent of press releases and plug your information in.

Like the copy for your website and blog, be sure to be careful not to make any promises you know you can't keep and use fuzzy fear threats and vague salvation promises if necessary in your PR.

Once written, the next step is to shop your PR to the media sheep. A simple web search will give you e-mail addresses and phone numbers of the media contacts your need whether your market is local to your city, national in scope or a global domination of fear.

Once you've compiled a list of contacts (which you've done for free on the Internet) start spreading the news. Key to getting your e-mail PR read is to be very business-like in the Subject line. Things like "Save Your Penis from Embarrassing Shrinkage?" doesn't cut it. Try "Company Testing Permanent Solution to Erectile Dysfunction in Men." Sound medical, scientific and professional even if you're not. More business-like your presentation the better the response will be.

Then, a few days after you've sent your PR to all of your media contacts start the phone follow-up.

A simple call asking if the contact has received your news and if they have any questions is a non-threatening way to get your foot in the door of sensational news reporting.

- DO NOT BE SHY!
- DO NOT BE OBNOXIOUS (like using all caps)!
- DO NOT LIE!
- DO BE PERSISTENT!
- DO BE CONSISTENT!
- WHEN IN DOUBT, BE VAGUE!

Chapter 5: The STDs You Want – Get Socially Transferred Dollars for Free

A Word on Social Media DIY

Social media is the modern day equivalent of the movie *War of the Worlds* where a radio program caused riots and nationwide panic by lying about aliens landing who were about to conquer the earth.

Social media was built to spread fear and panic and has to be part of your overall fear-marketing plan.

But with so many techniques, technologies and tactics floating around how do you put social media to work for you and where do you start?

Read on my friend, we'll get you going.

Step 1: Pick a Poison to Experiment With

Don't get intimidated or confused by the plethora of websites and social media outlets available. From Twitter, FaceBook, Pinterest, Google+, Instagram and YouTube pick one to get to know and to start with. By choosing one social media outlet at a time you can focus and understand it and then expand to the others.

Set Time Management Parameters

Getting sucked into the social media world happens all the time and before long you'll find yourself in a dark room with the curtains closed at 3 a.m. talking with other freaks just like you online. And this time it's not online self-enjoyment time like when you type with one hand and with your other hand you...

Remember that social media is just one additional outlet in your fear-marketing campaign and that the time and energy to understand it and use it effectively must be tempered with dedication to the other aspects of your overall fear marketing plan.

Or, hire someone to do it for you. If you're an idiot on the computer it may be money well spent. You make the honest call on your proficiency.

Establish Social Media Goals

What do you want out of social media? Traffic to your website? Widespread panic? Sales-sales-sales?

Set realistic goals. Set your specific social media outlets into motion. Track results and tweak your social marketing outlets and messaging as needed to meet your goals.

Create a Consistent Company Profile Across All Social Media Channels

Each social media site will want to include a profile on you, your company and your products/services. While some ask for basic information, others, such as FaceBook and LinkedIn also may allow you to include a bio, website links, blog entries, your photo and more.

Completing these profiles is critical and consistency is key when it comes to social media, especially as you expand across multiple sites. It's also crucial to keep your data consistent which will foster familiarity, reach, recognition and open communication with viewers, contacts and future customers.

Experiment and Tweak as Needed

Social media marketing is a fluid activity and allows you to experiment until you gets things right and figure out how to best spread your solution to people's greatest fears.

As you try different things it's either feast or famine on sales which is your real-world barometer on whether you are doing things right or not.

You product is bold. Your fear/solution is bold. Don't be afraid to throw your shit against the fan to see what sticks.

Chapter 6: It's a Swindle. Stealing The Infomercial Blueprint on Fear

While there are many easier marketing tools instead of the ubiquitous infomercial at your disposal, there are also lessons to be learned by watching the process by which successful infomercials spread fear, get attention and generate sales.

To drive enough fear and dread into your prospective customer to motivate them to buy your product let's steal some of the infomercial's greatest marketing hits.

Be the hero – Take a problem, make it worse, then save the day:

There is a basic understanding in everyday fear marketing to define a problem, make it worse and then solve the problem – for a price.

This concept has been around forever because it works and the infomercial world has sharper it finer than your geek office manager's needledick.

But how can you apply this motivating juggernaut throughout your marketing messaging and images? By first defining, and then driving the pain/pain relief process. Here you are making a direct connection because you are on the side of your customer and ready to help where they need is most (as defined by you).

Show how you've helped people just like them solve the same fear:

Testimonials, case studies and trotting people out who are just like the customers you want to reach have been a mainstay in great infomercials.

Why? Because nothing is more convincing than "hey, that fucking goober has a shirt just like mine and if this product works for him it can really work me."

These commonality-driven marketing messages enable the prospect to see how great life will be if they use your product or service.

Testimonials can overcome objections and illustrate benefits through a recognizable, personal story. If you have no legitimate testimonials, that's what friends and family are for.

Again, when in doubt be vague.

Repeat the fears. Rinse with solutions. Repeat the fears. Reap the benefits:

The best infomercials are never shy at driving the fears through the brains of the viewers and then repeating the benefits and call to action over and over and over and over again.

Why? Because it fucking works! To keep your audience's attention present the fears multiple times then restate the benefits over and over again and finally close from a variety of calls to action that all basically say the same thing. Buy now or die!

Create urgency, generate action:

Regardless of how great your product is if there is not an immediate motivating factor for people to buy now and right now they will put it off until tomorrow and you've lost them forever. It's up to you and your messaging to demonstrate why they need you and need you now.

THEY WILL DIE IF THEY DON"T BUY!

Call to action. Call to action. Call to action:

A.B.C. Always. Be. Closing. Repeat that a thousand times in your mind. Without it, you are the one who's dead – dead broke as a joke. By creating a clear and easy reason and way for the customer to buy and buy right now you are utilizing successful Marketing 101.

Tell your audience to take a specific action – Call Now. Here's the number. Click Here to Order.

Tell them exactly what to do and what will happen next. Infomercials handle this through repetition (see, you know it works) by repeating the phone number or website or catchphrase so much it becomes etched into their psyche.

This is not the time to be timid.

If your overall marketing message resonates with your prospects then a hard hitting call to action will be money in your pocket.

Chapter 7: Be Funny, Be Poor

Was it funny when your dog got off his cheap leash and was hit by a truck while you watched a kid?

Fuck no!

Funny when the grandpa who gave you a dollar every birthday fell down a dimly lit flight of stairs, broke his neck and finally died after hours alone on the floor?

No so much.

Fear/solution marketing and humor don't mix so keep away from the funny in your message. Remember that you're making things look as bad as possible to make your solution look as great and necessary as possible.

According to industry studies one out of every five TV ads are funny with ads running during sporting events, such as the Super Bowl ads, are three times funnier than the rest. But do they move product?

For your product marketing, based on creating fear and then solving the worst problems, the money thrown away on humor means nothing.

This is because the same industry research found that neither Super Bowl ads nor funny ads work better than other marketing angles.

Humorous marketing does gain attention but fear marketing gets remembered. While funny ads can get laughs and make people smile, your ads get gasps by showing people the worst that can happen and then get sales by showing how your product and your product only can remedy the problem.

Laughs and sales are not related.

Chapter 8: Pain and Sex and Death: I'll Buy

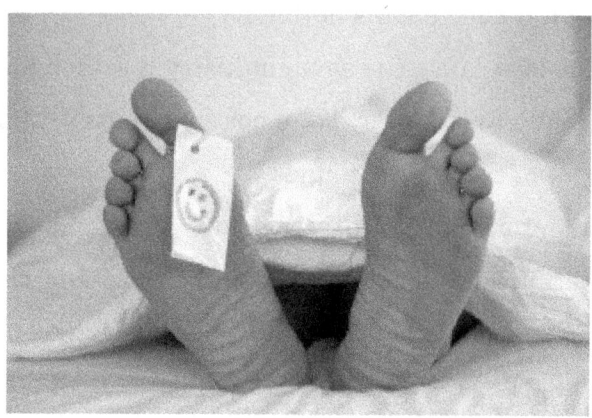

Regardless of what your product is or what it does it can be messaged to solve major fears – both real and created – in the areas that trigger the most intense responses in the human creature: Pain, Sex and Death.

How can you create and design a product to solve the biggest fears that are the major human flashpoints? Let's start by defining the major dreads and you can use your imagination on where you and your heaven-sent product can fit in.

PAIN

Because pain can be caused by a variety of internal and external impacts on the human body, the slate is wide open on how your product/service may help.

Which of the following maladies scare you the most and, if there was a magic elixir to solve them, would you buy it?

- Carpal Tunnel Syndrome
- Abdominal Pain: From a mild stomach ache to cramps, abdominal pain can be caused by almost anything – how can you help?
- Hip Pain: Especially with athletes and the elderly, the hip joint can become painful as cartilage wears down. Pretty universal pain to come to the rescue of.
- Knee and Joint Pain: Please see hip pain and add arthritic pain to the mix.
- Back Pain: Ahh, the holy grail of pain with hard to pinpoint causes. How can your product shine? Causes can be accidents, muscle strains, sports injuries and more. Jackpot!
- Neck and Shoulder Pain: Think joint and muscle issues and cash in. Also think whiplash for an automotive twist.
- Muscle Pain: Everyone's had it at one time or another. Another universal problem will pay to solve.
- Depression Pain: Sad to say.

How can your product reduce pain (not eliminate –
see the chapter on false advertising and the FTC).

SEX

Now on to the good stuff. Not as universal as the fear
that pain can generate but a close second, sexual
problems are often more perceived than real but that
does not diminish the enormous cash flow possibilities if
you can solve their problems in the sack and/or with
their sacks.

What issues can you solve (for the right price plus
free shipping)?

SEXUAL PROBLEMS/SOLUTIONS: MEN

Ahh… rugged masculinity (Brokeback Mountain-
style or traditional). When Johnsonly challenged,
especially in their Underoos, men get very serious, very
quickly. Whether they are getting busy once a day, once
a year, or just getting busy by themselves, when a man
has issues with his twig and berries it becomes an issue
to be addressed immediately.

Eureka! YOUR SOLUTION TO THE RESCUE!

Let's review some of the major pain points for the
sexually-challenged male and how your solution can
help.

Remember, it doesn't have to be a pill or cream, it
can be mental or physical exercises or anything else.

- Premature Ejaculation: Stats show that one in three men are too quick on the draw. "Whoooops! Sorry honey." Will your yoga exercises help?

- Not Interested Anymore: The libido don't work no good no more. What can your woman use to get your motor running again? Why we have just the product. Here's how and why she needs to buy it right now...

- Erection Go Bye Bye: Ahh, the little blue pill, or... , your special elixir to get the old redwood going. Viagra, Levitra, and Cialis make billions but are not safe for everyone. Is your ancient Chinese secret, pill or exercise, even though it's not FDA approved, the ticket to reach the thicket? The right fear-based marketing campaign could beat the stiffest competition.

- Low Testosterone: Sing along now – "I'm half the man I used to be..." Testosterone truly is the most important male hormone.
It helps to maintain sex drive, sperm production, muscle, and bone mass. There are no shortage of Low T remedies.
What's your solution? Be sure to say "Not FDA approved."
Be sure to include the benefits of combating Low

T including that it can cause erection problems, muscle loss and a diminished sex drive. Three issues solved at once. Huzzah!

SEXUAL PROBLEMS/SOLUTIONS: WOMEN

Now this may be an area where you market a man's biggest fear to shock the fuck out of a potentially apathetic female market.

If she's not into the wild thing anymore he may go-a-roaming. Which problems can you exploit that will trigger a man and/or woman to buy before he flies?

When a woman has a low sex drive or trouble having an orgasm, the medical community says that they have female sexual dysfunction, also called FSD.

Types of FSD include:

- Low sex desire
- Issues becoming aroused
- Trouble having an orgasm.
- Pain during sex.

If you can show the woman (or her partner) that she may be more than just tired or have a headache, how you can help, and how this will keep her relationship together you may have just gotten a great customer.

Be The Solution

Whatever your product is or what it does can it be messaged to solve the most intense fears in the human creature: Pain, Sex and Death?

How can you apply your product to solve the biggest human fear?

DEATH

Nothing more scary than death. It's the best in the business when it comes to creating human fear whether you believe you'll go to heaven, get seven virgins or just be burned into a crappy urn that will be stored in the back of someone's closet.

But regardless of belief, everyone thinks about death and that creates a fertile market for your fear-based marketing message. The following death probability statistics were gleaned from a variety of sources including The National Center for Health Statistics, The National Safety Council and the World Health Organization.

First, how can you convince your customer to think that they will die in one of the following ways, and, secondly, how can you market your product to be their savior?

Death? I hear you knocking but you can't come in...

- Fireworks Discharge (1-in-615,488): Every year in the United States about 10,000 people a year in the U.S. are admitted to hospital emergency rooms.

- Tsunami (1-in-500,000): Yep, the Big Kahuna of waves itself. Maybe not so much the U.S. but the global market is listening.

- Dog Attack (1-in-147,717): Bad dog! Bad dog! Stats show that just behind your fellow humankind snuffing you out is a little puppy just waiting to get the biggest kibble of his doggy life.

- Earthquake (1-in-131,890): California residents – hello?!?

- Snake, Bee or Venomous Bite (1-in-100,000): 50 people a year die in the U.S. every year. I say a Bzzz Bzzz Bzzz!

- Lightning Strike (1-in-83,930): Shocking! Yeah, I know, that was pretty bad.

- Tornado (1-in-60,000): Auntie Em! Auntie Em!

- Legal Execution (1-in-58,618): Bad Boys, Bad Boys...

- Flood (1-in-30,000): If you see a boat delivering the mail you're in trouble.

- Air Travel (1-in-20,000): Make sure your frequent flyer miles are in the Living Trust.

- Drowning (1-in-8,942): The World Health Organization says that drowning is the third leading cause of unintentional death worldwide. Do you have the arm floaties to save humanity?

- Electrocution (1-in-5,000): Shocking! Sorry, flogging a dead horse of a joke.

- Bike Accident (1-in-4,717): I don't want to ride my bicycle...

- Natural Forces (1-in-3,357): The wrath of God. Flood, earthquake, lightning or your girlfriend's mother's beef stroganoff. Equally deadly.

- Fire or Smoke (1-in-1,116): Sorry, I can't find this one funny for personal reasons.

- Shot by Firearm (1-in-325): Rat-a-tat-tat. Murder capital unless you're protected with our product.

- Falling Down (1-in-246): See one of the best fear-based marketing ads in history: "I've fallen, and I can't get up." There's a reason why it's still selling after decades.

- Suicide (1-in-121): Hit the pre-emptive solution marketing answer. Look for signs, etc. Every 40 seconds someone somewhere kills themselves. Sorry, no repeat business.

- Motor Vehicle Accident (1-in-100): Look twice before proceeding.

- Personal Accidents (1-in-36): Watch that banana peel. This is a very fertile ground for problem solving products.

- Stroke (1-in-23): Your lifestyle changing product solutions to the rescue? Watch that second helping of red meat.
- Cancer (1-in-7): See the Truth.com marketing campaign for successful hints on marketing that works.
- Heart Disease (1-in-5): See Stroke above.

Everyone, everywhere is concerned about death.

How can you create and market a product to be their savior?

Chapter 9: The Kings of Fear: The Charities

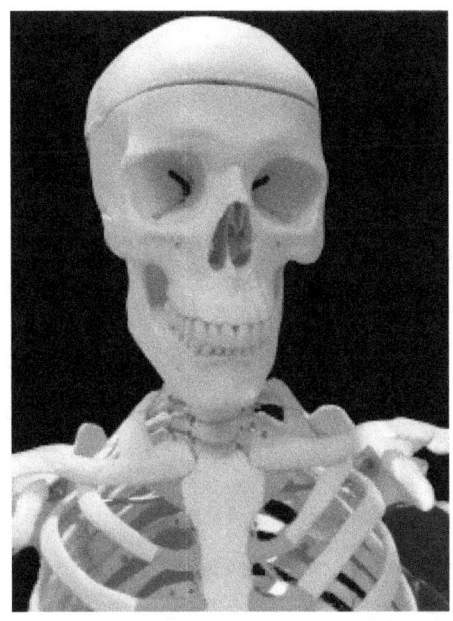

"Please give so I can live.
Oh fuck, you're too late dickhead..."

We've all seen it. The starving kid with flies all over his face. The brown, dried crops. The hobo freezing in the snowstorm. The emaciated dog at the kennel of horror. No water in the village. Are they legit? For the most part I think so. But even if they aren't they're effective.

So who's behind these messages that you remember even if you turn away within seconds. They are the kings of fear-based marketing. They are the charities.

But with so much marketing clutter attacking Mr. and Mrs. John Q. Consumer (aka The Gullibles) how do the charities bust through and convince you to part with you hard earned money without delivering any shred of provable results or tangible payback to you.

When you pay for an orange, you get an orange in your hand to eat. That's a tangible payback and deliciously juicy as well.

But a charity is a different beast. How do you know that your donated dollar is really helping that poor fucking kid living in a cow dung hut?

The truth is that even with the most stringent government oversight you don't know for certain if your money is buying a meal for a needy person or just another shrimp cocktail at the charity's annual board of directors' meeting.

This is where creating guilt and fear is king. This is marketing fear charity-style. It's a basic human reaction that is inherent in all people. The more disturbing the image, the more disgusting the message, the more dire the potential outcome, the better the response.

Like it or not the wallet is often opened just to dispell revulsion and/or disgust which translates into a full till for the charity.

They want your money and know how to get it. Let's give marketing props where props are due.

But some people think the charities go beyond the limit of acceptable images and donation-wrenching messaging. The distressing content designed to make all people feel upset or guilty, which hits kids especially hard, continues to turn off a percentage of the giving public who felt unjustly and disgustedly pressured to donate.

But the truth is that charities don't care about that segment of the donating public anyway. They need donations as their lifeblood and will use the most effective marketing messages to get into your wallet.

How Charities Market for Money

Make no mistake that charities are some of the most sophisticated, creative and proficient marketers on earth. Their marketing tactics share much with for-profit companies with a definite sway toward the emotive message.

Tug at the heart strings and strum the purse strings. Here's how they do it:

- **Tools of the trade:** Online fundraising is a proven winner to get donations (just ask any politician beginning with Obama).

Charities embrace mobile marketing for a reason
– it works. It works because they have created
not only the mobile messaging but also donation
capturing tools that work across all mobile
platforms.

- **You don't get if you don't ask:** Doesn't matter
  how many people look at a TV ad or visit a
  website. Eyes don't directly equate to revenue.
  Charities know – and you can put this to work in
  your online and mobile marketing – that if you
  get people to your website you have to make
  them act. Charities do this by drawing attention
  through precise design to their "donate now"
  button. You can't miss it.

Every charity website worth its beans has a
gigantic and undeniable "donate now" button.
And when people click and get to the donation
form that page is designed with ultimate
simplicity in mind.

Again, sending your money should be as easy as
possible for you. On the donations page you'll
often find that the website navigation graphics
have been removed along with columns, search
and any graphic notices.

Does you product order page deliver such simplicity?

- **The charity is the brand:** A recognizable brand instills confidence in the donor, meaning customer. Charities, like your company, should be fully branded across all marketing channels reinforcing name, logo, and imagery and copy that drives brand consistency. Charities do this to help donors feel secure giving their money to someone they trust.

- **Give and give often:** Getting a one-time donation or customer purchase is swell but what's even better? Captive and repeat business. Charities are king at marketing for steady income streams. You can be king of marketing for steady and repeat customer purchases with the approaches defined in this book.

- **Seize the moment:** Charities are king at capitalizing on the latest tragedy. The moment something tragic happens is the best opportunity for someone to donate because it is front and center in people's minds.

How can you attach your product to give the perception that you are helping those in need?

Now is not the time to be timid.

Now is the time to act!

Charities first define an emotion or fear to the public to gain their attention and then show donors/customers how their money will be used as remedy – they want to know how you, with their help, have made the world a better place.

These are tools you can put to work in your marketing message.

As we talked about earlier – create the fear and then be the savior with the solution to make everything all right.

Chapter 10: Can You Go Too Far?

What's wrong and what's right? Fear/Solution or just disgusting? Can you go too far? Yep.

Not fear-based marketing but I love the absolute disregard to basic parenting this ad represents. Doesn't matter the era – wrong is just wrong.

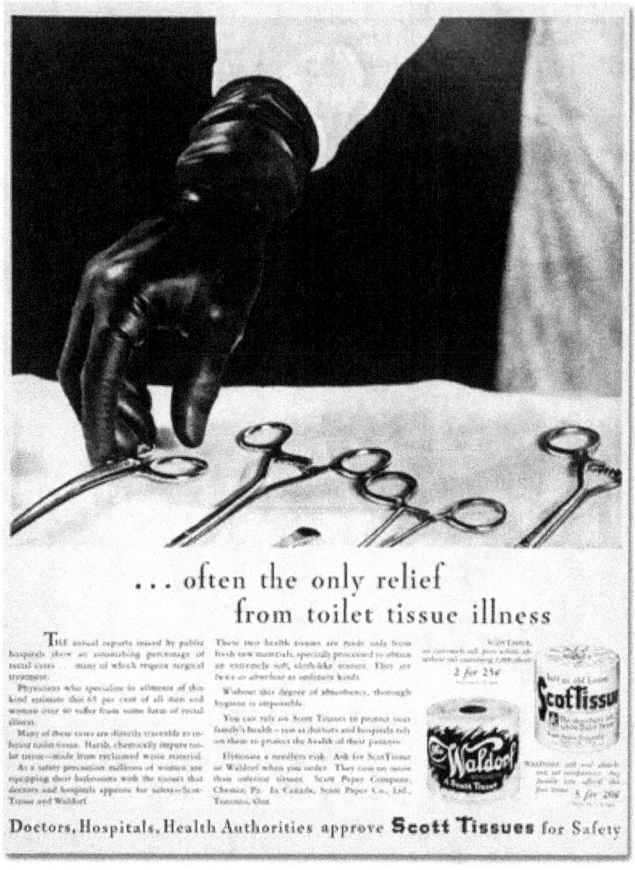

... often the only relief from toilet tissue illness

Doctors, Hospitals, Health Authorities approve **Scott Tissues** for Safety

Now this is a good one because it touches on the basic fears and everyday events that we all share.

- Everyone shits.
- Everyone wipes.
- Most wipe with cheap toilet paper.
- Anal surgery is scary and something no one (well almost no one) wants to experience.

Another good one.

Basic bodily function fears we all share resonates with all customers. Here is the fear of dropping mud at the worst time. The fear is created and the solution in delivered. No bubbling brown town for that guy or his ladies.

Now this one is a bit tough. The idea of the ad is spelled out clearly in the title:

"Don't treat others the way you don't want to be treated."

The problem is that the animal rights and protection group that ran the ad may have gone a bit far because while they equate killing animal babies to killing human babies. No dad or mom wants to see a fucking dead and bleeding baby.

This ad creates only fear and the only fear they're showing is that of scary animal. The first thing I thought about was that if I killed that animal when it was a baby my human baby may have lived. Backfire on the message.

Don't buy exotic animal souvenirs

Emotional appeals to the fear button are very common by charity and relief organizations, especially animal rights groups.

This print ad highlights a fear that is already known and suggests that the viewer can provide the solution. Meaning that when you buy exotic animal products you are spilling blood unnecessarily so don't buy them.

I give this an average grade because most people actually don't travel the world looking for exotic animal pelts. But for the specific audience that does this one's not too bad.

And the Coup De Grace...

Dying of Cancer? Fuck You. My Cancer is Worse.

When is direct, bold and water-cooler-banter-driven emotional advertising at it's most controversial? When you pit one death against another.

"Anything your cancer can do mine can to better."

As we talked about earlier charity advertising is very competitive and very challenging. It is a huge business with a limited pool of donors.

It looks like what the people behind this pancreatic ad campaign did was to try to cut through the marketing noise via dramatic impact, shock and guilt which they have weighed as equally important as emotion, sympathy and appeal in their messaging.

This campaign, which basically said that you've gotten off light and are extremely lucky to just have cancer and not pancreatic cancer, was intentionally created to stir things up. At its core it's an emotionally charged shock ad.

A success? It depends on whom you ask. So let's ask the basic Marketing 101 questions:

- **Was it offensive?** Well, yes. Yes, it was deeply offensive to those who have cancer but not pancreatic cancer.

  Say you have lung cancer, breast cancer or another cancer that came about naturally and not through lifestyle choices. Are you happy with the ads? Probably not. There is no good cancer.

- **Was it effective?** Well, although the campaign was pulled from the public domain for a reason, it created buzz because for as many people who liked it was the same amount of people who were offended by it.

The result? People on both sides of the aisle were talking about it. The ads did do their job which was to create buzz and dialog. Mission accomplished.

- **Did it do more harm than good?** The breast cancer people may say yes while the pancreatic cancer side says no.

  The ads created an air of divisiveness by ranking one cancer more important than another. Seems like in the cancer donation business this can be counter-productive, insensitive and simply turn people off to the entire thought of giving anything.

  But desperation sometimes drive drastic action and the shock ads that the campaign used did get attention both good and bad.

Is this a successful campaign? Again, depends on whom you ask.

Chapter Last: Start Fear Today Boys and Girls

Have a beer with fear!

Create their worst fear, dread and panic in pictures, scenarios and soundtrack. Then deliver happy calm and smiles through your instant solutions. Only thing to do next is to roll that wheelbarrow of cash to your mattress.

Their worst fear is helplessness. Death is under their bed while they're unable to move. There really is a monster inside your child's closet or lunchbox. The fears you just made them feel are very, very real (maybe) and ready and waiting to fuck their life to the core.

"But wait! We can solve all your problems…"

www.ingramcontent.com/pod-product-compliance
Lightning Source LLC
Chambersburg PA
CBHW071801170526
45167CB00003B/1120